301 STYLISH STORAGE IDEAS

Better Homes and Gardens® Books
Des Moines, Iowa

Better Homes and Gardens® Books
An imprint of Meredith® Books

301 Stylish Storage Ideas
Editor: Linda Hallam
Contributing Editors: Paula Marshall, Heather Lobdell, Joetta Moulden, Elaine Markoutsas,
  Tangi Schaapveld
Art Director: Jerry J. Rank
Copy Chief: Catherine Hamrick
Copy and Production Editor: Terri Fredrickson
Contributing Copy Editor: Sara Bonnassin
Contributing Proofreaders: Carol Boker, Martha Long, Jo Ellyn Witke
Electronic Production Coordinator: Paula Forest
Editorial and Design Assistants: Kaye Chabot, Judy Bailey, Treesa Landry, Karen Schirm
Production Director: Douglas M. Johnston
Production Manager: Pam Kvitne
Assistant Prepress Manager: Marjorie J. Schenkelberg

Meredith® Books
Editor in Chief: James D. Blume
Design Director: Matt Strelecki
Managing Editor: Gregory H. Kayko
Executive Shelter Editor: Denise L. Caringer

Director, Sales & Marketing, Retail: Michael A. Peterson
Director, Sales & Marketing, Special Markets: Rita McMullen
Director, Sales & Marketing, Home & Garden Center Channel: Ray Wolf
Director, Operations: George A. Susral

Vice President, General Manager: Jamie L. Martin

Better Homes and Gardens® Magazine
Editor in Chief: Jean LemMon
Executive Interior Design Editor: Sandra S. Soria
Executive Building Editor: Joan McCloskey

Meredith Publishing Group
President, Publishing Group: Christopher M. Little
Vice President, Consumer Marketing & Development: Hal Oringer

Meredith Corporation
Chairman and Chief Executive Officer: William T. Kerr

Chairman of the Executive Committee: E. T. Meredith III

Cover Photograph by Susan Gilmore. The room shown is on page 73.

All of us at Better Homes and Gardens® Books are dedicated to providing you with information and ideas
to enhance your home. We welcome your comments and suggestions. Write to us at: *Better Homes and
Gardens®* Books, Shelter Editorial Department, 1716 Locust St., Des Moines, IA 50309-3023.

If you would like to order additional copies of any of our books, check with your local bookstore.

301 STYLISH STORAGE IDEAS
CONTENTS

LIKE LOVE AND MONEY, STORAGE IS HARD to have too much of—and often hard to find. To make the most of potential storage, think beyond the walls of individual rooms, shelves, and closets to every available inch. With planning, storage works as part of your overall design, adding to the style as well as the function of every room in your home.

Whether furniture-quality cabinetry and built-ins or stylish and instant retail solutions meet your needs, you'll find inspiration and practical tips in these five chapters. Start with

ALL AROUND THE HOUSE

Chapter 1 for planning whole-house solutions; turn to Chapters 2 through 5 for room-by-room approaches. To make it easy to find what you need, tips are numbered 1 through 301.

Because his kitchen opens to the dining and living areas, opposite, architect Charles Aquino designed cherry cabinets that emulate the detailing and finishes of furniture. Raised paneling and cornice molding enhance the subtle Arts and Crafts period style.

ALL AROUND THE HOUSE
THE BUNGALOW

When Mike and Marge Walsh planned their new Mahtomedi, Minnesota, house, they wanted a comfortable, stylish kitchen. And they wanted their goals met in a convenient space open to both the breakfast and dining areas. Working with architect Tod Drescher and cabinetmaker Dave Griffin, Mike and Marge found well-planned storage helped minimize square footage while maximizing style.

With the kitchen properly consolidated in 9x12 square feet, the plan includes a tucked-away baking center and both top and base cabinets on the three walls of the U-shaped plan. For more storage, the architect and cabinetmaker incorporated the built-in breakfast bar with base storage, a shallow china cabinet for glassware, and a handsomely crafted, generously-scaled sideboard. The built-ins take advantage of every bit of space, allowing the compact plan to function for family living and for entertaining. The china cabinet, on the side wall of the built-in refrigerator, opens to the dining area and uses, at a depth of just 8 inches, a blank wall that is often wasted. And the illumininated glassware warms the space as a decorative element.

The sideboard works particularly well, adding needed storage for china, serving pieces, and flatware. It also functions as a server for family meals, dinner parties, and casual, buffet-style entertaining. Marge had the sideboard built in to reflect the light maple used throughout the open house. The sideboard, measuring 16 inches deep by 94 inches wide by 36 inches high, is comparatively sized to standard pieces. Although Marge chose to have the interior fitted with shelves because china storage was her primary concern, such custom pieces are often designed and built with specialized storage including racks for linens, drawers for serving pieces, or vertical dividers for oversized trays.

1 Use every inch—even every six inches, (right). That's how deep the useful and attractive shelves are in this built-in that takes the place of a conventional small china cabinet. For an open, contemporary look, have shelves cut from glass and include interior lighting.

2 Have fun with the space under a built-in table (right). Here, this often-neglected space doubles as a wine rack constructed from custom milled 1 1/16 x 1 1/16 maple strips. Each rack is 4 7/16 inches wide between slats.

3 Think of kitchen cabinets (right) as fine furniture and treat accordingly. These custom ones are maple, finished with coats of flat and low luster semigloss polyurethane by the cabinetmaker so the wood retains its light color and clear finish.

4 Combine storage (above) with any built-in dining table, banquette unit, or breakfast bar. Note the toaster cover on the granite tabletop and the wine rack below are made of maple strips.

5 Personalize your storage needs to reflect your culinary interests. The baking center (right) contains all the necessary equipment, ingredients, and supplies in one convenient place. A combination of open shelves and drawers helps organize supplies and equipment.

6 Use bifold doors (right) for a storage area, such as the baking center, that's accessible.

7 Before planning a major built-in piece, such as a sideboard (above) or built-in cupboard, measure a freestanding piece that accommodates your storage needs. Measure the space where the built-in will be placed to make sure it will fit without overpowering.

8 Consider visual continuity from room to room when working with storage in new construction or a major remodeling. The sideboard (above) is in the same style, wood, and finish as the custom cabinets because the dining and kitchen areas open to each other. Note, too, the custom, handcrafted pulls that match all cabinetry in the kitchen and dining areas.

9 If you like the idea of mixing woods or finishes, introduce two stains (light and dark, for example) on the kitchen wall and base cabinets. Choose one stain for built-ins in the adjacent dining area.

ALL AROUND THE HOUSE
THE RANCH

When a top-to-bottom remodeling gave this 30-year-old suburban ranch-style house an updated look, improved storage played a leading role. The owners first worked with their designer to assess how they lived in their home—and where they needed open and concealed storage. They

started with the family's gathering place. The family room didn't provide storage for their big screen television, and it was devoid of bookshelves and even rudimentary shelving for electronic equipment. To free up floor space for a media center, the designer first moved the basement steps. This added square footage that converted neatly into the closet, which can be closed off with attractive, louvered bi-fold doors. The attention to more stylish built-ins carried over to the kitchen. By eliminating a little-used breakfast area, the kitchen gained extra space for wall-mounted and base cabinets and touches such as the bar area for parties.

13 Combine solid panel and glass-door cabinets (above) for the most options in open and concealed storage. Cabinets here are maple.

14 Even in a generously sized kitchen you can use often-wasted space. Mount wall ovens (above) high enough to allow a deep drawer for broiling pans, pizza pans, and cookie sheets.

15 Incorporate curved cabinet doors for a peninsula (above and left) or an island. Items are accessible immediately with this door arrangement.

16 If you entertain frequently, turn one cabinet into a wine rack (left). Use drawers for bar equipment, such as corkscrews. If space allows, consider adding a small refrigerator, ice maker, or refrigerated cooler for white wine storage at the optimum temperature.

10 Consolidate your electronic equipment with one storage cabinet (above left). Louvered doors are ideal, as they allow air circulation for electronics.

11 A closet storage system, with cabinets suspended from a wall-mounted track (above left) allows flexibility in shelving,

which can be easily reconfigured. Check home centers and specialty closet companies for specific brands.

12 For economical and stylish shelving with the look of custom built-ins (above left), use a closet system for bookcases, too. Units are normally prefinished.

THE NEW
TWO STORY

With 1,800 square feet and no basement or attic, this Michigan lake house offered the challenge of melding storage with contemporary style. The openness of the plan and the owners' desire for a sleek, uncluttered look also dictated hiding the essentials of daily life—accessible, but understated storage as background to the stunning views and sleek, modern furnishings.

The program begins in the entry, where architect Ken Neumann of Neumann/Smith Associates in Detroit designed an intricate, pull-out dining table that stores into the sideboard (see page 15). This entry/dining hall opens to the storage-oriented living area, where a wall of discreet maple cabinets surrounds the fireplace. For a smooth wall and virtually concealed storage of electronic equipment, hidden-touch latches take the place of levers, knobs, or pulls. With curved, maple-trimmed shelves for art display, a divider wall between the living area and kitchen wraps around the stairs to the upper level and introduces the cabinetry in the equally contemporary work spaces beyond.

As the kitchen is visible easily from the entrance, the owners preferred clean lines and sleek storage for necessities. They accomplished this with custom maple cabinets, mirroring the style of the living room cabinets,

17 Plan during the design phase of your project to incorporate concealed storage. In the living room (opposite), *touch-latch natural maple cabinets house the electronic equipment in the fireplace wall.*

18 For the ultimate in hidden storage with high style, the glass-topped coffee table (opposite) *houses the projection television. The large screen rolls down discreetly from a slot in the ceiling above the fireplace.*

19 Use a section of open, gently curved display shelves (left) *to transform a wall of cabinetry into a design focal point. For added interest, the dark bubinga wood is trimmed with the same pale maple used for the living room and kitchen storage cabinets.*

and exotic bubinga wood as the wall that contains the refrigerator and related storage. The dishwasher is hidden discreetly behind a maple cabinet door while drawer fronts blend seamlessly into the fine woods. Because of space limitations, the washer and dryer are tucked behind cabinet doors in the kitchen.

If you prefer your contemporary design in crisp white, work with a cabinet shop for a smooth lacquer or tough enamel finish. Laminate, fused to a material such as particleboard, translates well into stylish surfaces if you like the look of all-white or colorful cabinets. For inside and out durability, cabinet doors should be laminate-clad. It's a good solution for a heavy-use family kitchen, as prints wipe off with a damp sponge.

24 Incorporate recessed lighting into your built-in display cabinets (opposite). Pure white halogen lighting, which doesn't distort colors, often is used to illuminate art glass.

25 Combine light and dark woods for stylish kitchen cabinets (center). Here exotic bubinga wood clads the refrigerator wall while lighter maple is used for the upper and base kitchen cabinets, including the dishwasher. For another look, use the dark wood to visually anchor the base cabinets and pair with light wood for wall cabinets.

26 Take advantage of the space under windows to build in a handsome, space-saving sideboard with a pull-out, stored-away table (left and below). Extra leaves and folding chairs store.

20 Work with an experienced fine woodworker for projects as detailed and precise as this pull-out table (right). Get at least three to five references and look at projects on site to make sure you are satisfied with work quality.

21 If you prefer movable pieces, consider the possibility of having such a versatile sideboard/table combination crafted as a freestanding unit.

22 Take advantage of every bit of space for kitchen storage. A narrow cabinet (left) fits snugly between the window and the wall.

23 When space is tight, install cabinets from floor to ceiling as in this wall of storage around the concealed refrigerator (left). Band dark cabinets, here in bubinga wood, with a lighter wood, such as this pale maple, for detailing and architectural interest.

Equal care went into planning upstairs storage. The bedroom, with an open loft, is a study in melding high-style contemporary design and practical storage. With no space untapped, the architect designed deep drawers under the stairs to the loft and staggered a bank of drawers and open display cubes along the stairwell. The interior wall features a similar arrangement of stacked cubes and drawers for storage and display. The loft includes simpler, painted shelves on both ends and a desk constructed from file drawers.

27 Mix open display cubes with latch-touch cabinetry for a wall of bedroom built-ins (left). Stagger the arrangement for design interest and to allow space for art objects and prints.

28 With this much concealed storage, make a map so you'll remember where you've stored little-used items.

29 Use the stairwell for a wall of built-ins, such as the cubes (above), or for open, shallow shelving or display brackets. Choose colors and finishes that blend well between the living levels.

30 Think outside the box when you are desperate to add storage to a bedroom.

Headboard beds aren't what they used to be. Today, contemporary furniture stores offer designs that offer space-saving storage with style (left and right). If you can't find one you like, work with a custom furniture maker.

31 To stretch your storage budget, add plain painted plywood bookcases (right) either as built-ins or as freestanding units, in areas such as this loft.

32 Turn space under stairs (right) into oversized file drawers on sturdy tracks.

ALL AROUND THE HOUSE
THE TOWN HOUSE

Storage divides and conquers in this compact, 900-square-foot apartment above portrait painter Louis Brill's Richmond, Virginia, studio. "I liked the space because of the high ceiling, but it was actually quite small," he explains. "I don't like a lot of clutter so I knew it would be a challenge." For a solution, Louis turned to architect Charles Aquino, a master of putting style—and stylish storage—into tight places. (See pages 26 through 29 for Aquino's own apartment.)

"There literally wasn't enough square footage for separate rooms," Aquino adds. "Instead, I designed a series of storage areas to define the spaces. In most cases, the storage is what gives a space its identity. We thought of the town house as three units—the bedroom and bath, the living area, and the kitchen—and designed storage for each of those spaces. As Louis likes built-ins and didn't want a lot of open shelves, I was able to work in as much cabinetry as you find in many larger kitchens and family rooms."

In keeping with this idea, the architect used two identical peninsulas to define the kitchen within the open plan. (See photograph opposite and on page 21.) On the dining side, the cabinets store linens, china, silver, and table accessories, while on the living side the peninsula cabinets conveniently hold equipment and cookware. The solid back of the storage peninsula doubles as a half-wall for furniture that defines the sitting areas.

33 *When space allows in new construction or remodeling, flank a fireplace wall (opposite and left) with handsome storage cabinets.*

34 *Use detailing, such as the raised panel design, pilasters at the fireplace, and brass pulls (opposite and left) in the room style.*

35 *If you plan to paint your cabinets, stretch your budget by using medium-density fiberboard for the doors (opposite and left) rather than a solid wood such as cherry or maple. Paint-grade plywood is another option.*

36 *For the most storage possibilities, add a section or two of drawers behind cabinet doors. Depending on your needs, have drawers sized for videotapes, cassettes, or compact discs.*

37 *Explore stock or special-order home center cabinetry options. Depending on your space, stock cabinets can work well.*

As the centerpiece of the design, the fireplace wall works as a small library and home entertainment center. Aquino designed the mantel as integral with the decorative tops of the cabinets flanking the fireplace. This creates a strong horizontal line and integrates storage into the architectural design. As the town house is an open space without interior doors (except for the bathroom), the architect repeated the same simple raised panel design for the kitchen and living areas. Cabinets are 4 feet, 6 inches high in the living areas—creating a pleasing height. In living and family areas, Aquino often suggests drawers inside cabinets for easily accessible and organized storage. Open ¾-inch shelves, with 1¼-inch edging strips, are adjustable for oversized books, collections, and the owner's changing collection of art.

38 Plan built-ins (left) to handsomely hide your television and other electronic equipment . Measure the dimensions of the television, including the depth, before the plans are drawn. If you are buying a new television or other electronic equipment, such as stereo speakers, measure the pieces while you shop.

39 Adapt a television to a tall cabinet (left) with a custom swivel stand that pulls out for viewing. Incorporate a shelf to hold the VCR and tapes. Or, custom-size a cabinet unit to the television.

40 For easy viewing, have the television cabinet constructed so that the hinged doors slide back into the cabinet (left). Specify heavy-duty hinges so that the hardware will last.

41 When a peninsula or an island is accessible from two sides (right), install doors on both sides for access. The peninsula serves the kitchen and the dining areas.

42 Graduate the sizes of drawers (right) to increase storage possibilities. Use retail dividers to make the most of storage for your everyday flatware and small utensils and kitchen gadgets.

43 If you plan to store heavy items such as cast iron cookware, order durable heavy-duty drawer slides.

44 Install large drawers behind kitchen cabinet doors to avoid having to search for items such as pots or skillet tops. Size according to use.

45 Maximize storage by building cabinets to the ceiling (right). Store little-used items on the upper shelves. Step stools can be built into base cabinets.

No inch of living—or storage—space goes unused in this 900-square-foot Stillwater, Minnesota, condominium. And with good reason. Not only is it home to a busy professional couple, but it's also an office for the husband.

Originally classrooms in an old school, the unit is one of eight converted into living spaces. The first owners installed basics, including the kitchen, and saved a built-in that had been part of a classroom. They also built the boxed display shelves in the pass-through between the kitchen and dining area of the living room. Such simple shelving, constructed from lightweight plywood, is an economical and easy way to take advantage of what is essentially empty space. Even with this good start, the current owners definitely needed more open and concealed storage. Because of their interests and work, they designed and

46 *Use a pass-through (right) for extra display shelving. Construct such simple shelves with basic box construction—depth without weight.*

47 *In small kitchens (right), expand your storage options by hanging pots from boxed beams or conventional small-scale pot racks. Use the wall for additional storage, such as this decorative and functional arched metal rack from a kitchen shop.*

48 *Choose handsome versions of needed equipment so there's no need to store out of sight. The wall-hung measuring spoons, baskets, and cutting board (right) are decorative accessories as well as kitchen equipment.*

built additional storage for specific needs. In the living room, they used space under the window for a built-in that houses their extensive collection of compact discs. The shelves are crafted with 6-inch openings, perfectly sized to hold the CDs. The 19-inch depth allows a generous counter above to safely hold pottery pieces and electronic equipment. The same care went into the built-in bookcase designed around the window in the small home office/library/sitting room. Here, because space is truly at a premium, the shelves wrap the window from floor to ceiling. As the unit is the focal point of the room, it's painted a rich, deep purple that enhances the library feel. For interest, the adjustable shelves are placed at different heights. This allows for convenient storage of electronic

49 Waste no window. Maximize the opportunity to design and construct a built-in (above) or to introduce a low, freestanding storage unit or bench that holds books, plants, and other favorite accessories.

50 Plan built-ins for your own needs. The unit holds compact discs (above) for a music lover. But design in a measure of flexibility, too. Use adjustable shelves so heights can vary.

51 Make your shelves (above) deep enough to house oversized books and electronic equipment. These are 24 inches.

52 Plan your shelves for the kinds of books you collect and purchase (above). As different heights are more interesting, design lower shelves for larger volumes, such as college yearbooks and art books, and upper shelves for more standard sizes. If you have a collection of paperbacks, use a series of 8- to 10-inch shelves.

53 Open shelving (above) is more accessible and economical than cabinets. When neatly arranged, open shelves work in a home office/library. However, if you accumulate clutter, add baskets or boxes.

equipment as well as oversized books. The one closet in the room literally becomes the office, outfitted with a drawing board, upper shelves, a lower bin, and even a filing cabinet for papers and documents. Upper shelves are used to stock little-used items, and the wall doubles as a display board to hold drawing tools. Although the owner prefers to draw standing up, space under the drawing board could be used to tuck away a stool. When the double doors, with decorative handles, are closed, the office neatly converts into a sitting room/library. As an alternative to solid double doors, stock, bifold doors from a lumber yard or home center would provide another option for easy access and economical concealed storage.

54 In a small bath (above), *extend the vanity top to maximize shelf space for accessories and necessities.*

55 Use shaped bracket-type display shelves for bath storage (above). *Decorative accessory catalogs sell similar shelves, or they can be constructed by a finish carpenter or woodworker.*

56 Use decorative shelving and racks for towel storage (above). *A painted wooden shelf is another design option.*

57 Label plastic bins for low-cost, well-organized storage (left). *If you keep business papers or legal documents at home, invest in a fireproof cabinet or lockbox.*

ALL AROUND THE HOUSE
THE APARTMENT

For storage with a stylish edge, combine built-ins with freestanding pieces, advises architect Charles Aquino, whose own Richmond, Virginia, apartment is shown here and on pages 5, 28, and 29. "It was a completely unfinished space above my office," he says. "That gave me the opportunity to plan and design the built-ins I needed and to allocate wall space for my antique storage pieces."

When Aquino looks at space, for himself or for a client, he considers where built-ins work best and where he prefers to use antiques or other freestanding storage. "The kitchen is the obvious choice for cabinets," he says. "In some larger kitchens, I like to introduce a piece of furniture, such as a cupboard, but in smaller kitchens, built-in storage works best. When you do that, look for every

place you can use storage. Build above and around the refrigerator for a custom look that also adds cabinet space."

Other ideal spaces for built-ins include sitting areas, offices, stair landings, combination dining room/libraries, and bedrooms, Aquino says. "My apartment is too small for a dining room or a library in a real sense. But I was able to use the landing as a small library (see page 28). Most homes will have a blank wall or a window wall that could serve the same purpose."

Built-ins also work well in bedrooms, the architect adds, as they tend to be small rooms. "I work in a lot of older homes and town houses that were built before the days of the master suite. Even the largest bedrooms don't have a lot of floor and closet space. Shelves are a good way to take advantage of the wall. And built-in dressers free up floor space and eliminate the need for furniture. When possible, I like to do built-ins in the closets. That's a trend in new

58 *Shop for freestanding pieces that serve your storage and display needs* (opposite). *If you collect, consider pieces such as this plain-style Virginia cupboard with glass doors and concealed storage. If pieces are in the same scale and the woods blend, don't worry about mixing styles and periods.*

59 *Go with a classic* (opposite). *Sideboards combine storage opportunities. If you use yours for a bar, reinforce the drawers to support bottles.*

60 Take advantage of a blank wall. Maximize storage with floor-to-ceiling book shelves (opposite). Allow shelf depth of 12 inches clear on the inside, rather than the more common $10\frac{1}{2}$ to 11, so most books store with ease. Vary the heights for interest.

61 Consider the weight load. Architects often specify $\frac{3}{4}$-inch birch plywood for bookshelves. Restrict spans to 30 to 36 inches between supports. Reinforce every 24 inches if you use thinner plywood, such as $\frac{1}{2}$-inch.

62 Built-in chests or dressers (below) are ideal pieces that save space, especially if used in closets or dressing areas. Vary drawer depths for more storage options.

63 Size an open built-in (right) to house and support a small television in a bedroom or a playroom. Include convenient storage for the VCR and tapes.

construction that works in remodeling if your closet is large enough."

In rooms with more space options, Aquino suggests freestanding pieces that combine functions. "There was a reason for serving pieces, such as sideboards, to be designed as they were," he explains. "Originally, a sideboard was used to store china, silver, and linens all in one place and as a surface for serving food. Such pieces work quite well today, too. And they don't have to be particularly old to be interesting. I use an English Art Nouveau sideboard, probably from around 1880, in the hall adjacent to my dining area. Besides storage, it works great as a bar and a server when I have dinner or cocktail parties."

THE GARAGE APARTMENT

Above an English Tudor-style, two-car garage is a treasure of storage with style. It's also an18x18-foot, one-bedroom apartment that's home and office to Phil Long, a Tulsa, Oklahoma, special events planner. As a start, Phil left the two closets in place and used the space between for the twin bed that doubles as a daybed. The sleeping nook also

64 *When space is tight, stack graduated upholstered or papered boxes (above) for added storage with style. They hold napkins and other essentials. As an alternative, stack vintage suitcases.*

65 *Substitute a small antique chest (above) for a side table. As an alternative, shop thrift stores for 20th-century reproductions. Such pieces are good buys, as they often emulate the lines and basic style of the originals without the price tags. If you are using a chest*

to store silver, line drawers with cloth made to slow tarnishing. Use dividers to keep items handy.

66 *Choose every piece for its storage possibilities. For dining, use a writing table with a drawer (above). Depending on your needs, it can contain everything from flatware and linens to office supplies.*

67 *Use trunks wherever you can (above). For the most versatility, choose one with a flat rather than domed top, so that it can easily double as a table or*

functions as his television room as he had his television built into the wall (see below). The often-wasted, under-the-bed space adds extra storage, too. Other furniture and accessories work equally as well. In the dining area, the desk doubles as an eating table and home office with the fax machine located conveniently on an antique tin military trunk (more storage).

For the sitting area, a three-drawer French chest doubles as lamp shelf and side table. The low height is ideal, as the piece is placed in front of a window. On a solid wall, an antique bamboo secretary (not shown) stores essentials while collectibles and pictures are displayed on the upper shelves. "The most important considerations are scale and storage," says Phil. "I can truly say that every square foot is put to good use."

even a bench. Look at wicker trunks as readily available budget options.

68 Remember under-the-bed storage (above) when space is tight. Storage boxes and bins are ideal for out-of-season clothing and other items as well as extra bedding or magazines.

69 Start your storage at the front door. In a tiny entry, work with the scale and don't overpower with large pieces. A vintage hat rack (above right) is ideal not just for hats but also for shopping bags, lightweight jackets, and backpacks. If space allows, look at floor stands, too, for hats and coats. An umbrella stand is another convenient and practical storage organizer.

70 Don't overlook any surface when storage space is minimal. An extra decorative accent chair (above right) is ideal for holding a stack of books, decorating magazines, or even an accessory or plant. When you need an extra chair, it's close at hand, too.

IN TODAY'S OPEN, SHARED-SPACE STYLE, thoughtful storage creates practical and beautiful multipurpose rooms such as the dining room library here and on pages 34 and 35 and the library sitting rooms on pages 36 and 37. Much more than places to stash and store, the built-ins and freestanding pieces in these rooms are the backdrops for personal collections of furnishings, books, and art. Look for this blend of hardworking ideas and handsome design that you can translate into your own dining and living areas. And when you

LIVING AND DINING ROOMS

need storage help in a hurry, turn to "Quick Fixes," pages 56 and 57, for stylish, affordable, and instant retail solutions.

Designed for a family of readers and art collectors, this dining room library creates a warm, inviting backdrop for family dinners and night-time parties. Picture lights gracefully illuminate the painted bookshelves.

LIVE IN THE LIBRARY

When you love and collect books as well as art, why not live and dine in your library? With the help of Houston, Texas, architect Ed Eubanks, that's what this family does in a spacious room made all the more usable by four walls of built-in bookcases. "I don't judge a room by its size but by how the owners are going to use it and really live in it," Eubanks says. "Floor-to-ceiling bookshelves work well in larger rooms, but they can be equally effective in smaller spaces, too. The key is how they are integrated with windows and doors so the room and the storage work together and the shelves don't appear as an afterthought."

Here the built-ins flank French doors for storage as well as display. As the shelves are integral to the design of the room, Eubanks had them constructed from paint-grade wood and reinforced by edging strips. To accommodate oversized art and photography books, shelves measure 12 inches deep. Since the owners wanted a rich and light-filled space, the architect suggested a glazed finish rather than a dark stain. This yellow glaze, repeated for the woodwork in the room, sets the warm palette without overpowering. For interesting contrast, the back walls of the shelves are painted an equally warm and handsome terra-cotta shade in a flat finish.

When built-ins are literally the room, as in this case, extra detailing enriches the ambience. Here, Eubanks used a cornice molding around the tops of the shelves and the doors and a simple molding at the ceiling.

STORAGE OPTIONS

■ For a quick library, buy matching, stackable retail storage units or line up bookcases to fill the width of at least one wall. Stack for height.

■ Paint the interior back wall of an unfinished or vintage bookcase in a contrasting color to the exterior or shelves. Apply wallpaper cut to fit for another look.

■ Install floor-to-ceiling tracks on one or more walls in a family room or den. Have ¾-inch-thick, 10- to 12-inch-deep plywood planks cut to fit the wall and hang from adjustable shelf brackets.

71 For illumination with style, mount brass picture lights (opposite) above the top of bookshelves. Install one above every shelf and in corners for illumination.

72 To give bookshelves (opposite) the look of fine woodwork, select the same finish, here a glaze, for built-ins and trim.

73 Mix favorite art pieces, such as pottery and ceramics (opposite), with books for a warm feel in your library—and for safe display, too. In families with young children or young visitors, reserve the top shelves for breakables.

74 Hang a painting, print, or photograph from a vertical support (opposite) for prominent display. The piece immediately will take on importance. Choose an interesting frame for impact.

STORAGE OPTIONS

■ *Use stock molding and other stock detailing to trim basic built-ins or freestanding storage pieces. Look for such detailing at home centers and at specialty woodworking shops that carry reproduction trim.*

■ *Measure your love seat or sofa and have shelves built on either side for a recessed nook.*

■ *Think inside the box, too. Even rooms with flat, 8-foot ceilings have enough space for a bookshelf over the door. The same idea can work with wide cased openings, too. Make sure the spans are reinforced every 24 inches for support.*

■ *For closet-to-library conversion, remove the door and detail with new stock trim for a neat look; add shelves.*

75 *Match frames and mats when you hang artwork from a built-in (above). Choose art and picture frames that are compatible with the collectibles you are displaying safely on upper shelves.*

76 *Construct built-in bookshelves above paneled wainscoting (above) to create a pleasing backdrop for furniture.*

77 *Work with a cabinetmaker or finish carpenter to incorporate details, such as* vertical pilaster trim (above), when a built-in is used as fine furniture. Use color, such as the gold four-corner stars, to pick up applied detailing.

78 *Turn a cased opening between rooms into a mini library (right) with cabinets and open bookshelves. Even a narrow space adds valuable open and concealed storage.*

79 *Fit shelves to the slope of a vaulted ceiling (right). Use the centered wall space above* the door for extra display.

80 *Use your built-ins to stylishly frame other storage solutions (right). Here, a hat rack and umbrella stand in the adjacent entry hall provides more convenient and useful storage.*

81 *Think about color combinations. If you want your built-ins to stand out, contrast with the wall color. The mustard yellow walls (right) create a rich backdrop for the crisp white built-in shelves and cabinets.*

82 Extend built-in shelves to the ceiling (above) and trim with the crown molding for a finished, formal look. Create an extra tall (at least 18 inches high) display shelf to hang small art or photographs.

83 Transform a standard closet into a walk-in library (left) by replacing the door with a handsome arched opening trimmed with pilaster and keystone detailing.

84 Have shelving built floor-to-ceiling on all three walls (left) to maximize the found space with style.

ORGANIZE YOUR COLLECTIONS

The joy of collecting is living with what you love. When you have a passion for collecting, incorporate the objects of your desire into your rooms with appropriate storage. Depending on what you collect, consider whether built-ins or freestanding pieces, such as the pair of étagères, *below*, best meet your needs and budget. Also ponder carefully the style of what you collect and how it can be displayed to its best advantage. For example, use simple shelving for rustic or country objects. Add more detailing and refinements to shelves or bookcases if you collect porcelains used in more formal settings. And think about colors and finishes of shelves or furniture so your display will complement your collection, not compete with it.

■ **STORAGE OPTIONS**

■ *Think beyond the obvious for collection display. Look at a variety of pieces, such as metal baker's racks, which offer shelving options for your finds.*

■ *Buy your display pieces ready-made and already painted or stained. Accessory and decorating shops and home decorating catalogs sell a variety of shelves and brackets, including decorative ledges for family photographs. Measure your spaces and order to fit. Stack several shelves for the look and the display space you need.*

■ *Shop for a ready-made wall-mounted cabinet or a hanging corner cupboard. These are ideal for organizing a collection of small objects.*

85 For order and balance, use pairs, such as these étagères (left). Such open storage is ideal in a living room as the objects, rather than the display, are clearly visible. Note that each étagère displays a matching urn to strengthen the symmetry.

86 Adapt to the dimensions of furniture pieces by using books to elevate objects (left) that are small for the spaces. Place such pieces and other fragile objects out of the general traffic pattern.

87 Build in sturdy shelves (above) to display heavy collectibles such as these pottery pieces. Have such shelves built with ³⁄₄-inch plywood rather than ¹⁄₂-inch and reinforce with edging strips. Vary height and widths to accommodate your collectibles.

88 When possible, divide shelving into groups of three (above) as this odd number is more visually pleasing than even placement. For a strong focal point, install the top shelves or the top two levels at the same height.

89 Look for safe and visible display and storage for fragile or delicate art objects (right). Use the fireplace wall for a shallow display closet set between wall studs. If space allows, flank the fireplace to double the impact.

90 Reflect the beauty of your objects by mirroring the back wall (right). Install glass shelves so art appears to float in the space.

91 Install narrow French doors (right) so your collection can be seen and still be safe. If you have young children or young visitors, install locks on the doors. Incorporate recessed lighting in display units so objects can be illuminated dramatically at night.

STYLE AND YOUR TELEVISION

Style and your television aren't mutually exclusive. This is a good thing, because with today's open floor plans and multi-purpose rooms, the two often have to live side by side. If your television is in a media or family room, convenience and easy viewing, rather than total concealment, often are the priorities. But if it is in your main living area, discreetly convenient placement also becomes a design issue.

92 House a television in a cabinet (above) for a room divider between an open living and dining area. Here the doors face the living area in a town house with more style than size.

93 Maximize storage opportunities (above) by incorporating bench seating with storage into the television cabinet unit. For the simplest solution, have the bench crafted so the top lifts up. This is ideal storage for magazines, videocassettes, or table linens.

94 Be creative in small spaces. Instead of a space-grabbing sideboard, a serving ledge (above) in the dining room offers a contemporary alternative.

95 Go with a simple, practical solution. Size a wall of built-ins (left) with center space for a television on a pull-out swivel shelf. This works for televisions that are hard to see if placed in low cabinets.

96 Look for alternative places and ways to hide a television. If you have a stairwell adjacent to your living or sitting room (above) *transform the wasted space underneath into a pull-out shelf for your television and video cassette recorder.*

97 When space is extremely tight (above), *conceal with bifold, fold-back doors. And elevate the television for easier, more comfortable viewing.*

98 In an attic-type playroom, recess the television into the knee wall (above right). Build shelves into every nook and cranny, here around and above the door, to store other electronic equipment and tapes.

99 For a custom look in a true media room (right), work with an architect, designer, or cabinetmaker so the television fits precisely into the wall unit. Add open and closed storage.

■ STORAGE OPTIONS

■ *Adapt vintage, secondhand, or reproduction wardrobes or armoires as television cabinets. Measure your television, including the depth, before shopping for such a piece. Some storage pieces are too shallow to hold a television. Normally, the back of the unit will have to be drilled or cut for wiring, and well-supported shelves added.*

■ *Paint or stain an unfinished storage piece made for a television cabinet. These are normally for smaller sets; if you need a larger cabinet, adapt an unfinished storage cupboard or armoire-type piece with doors.*

100 *For design interest and storage options, vary the depth of your built-in sideboard, (above). This handsome piece is deeper in the center as a serving counter for buffets.*

101 *Place your built-in piece below a window and mirrored wall (above) for light. Choose a durable surface, here marble, for no-worry serving.*

102 *Use a built-in china cabinet (right) to define the dining room without blocking light. Glass doors on both sides keep the look light and open. Include cabinets for large trays.*

MAKE THE MOST OF YOUR DINING ROOM

And do it with storage solutions that enrich the style of the dining area—whether it is an elegant formal room or a casual spot off the kitchen. As a start, think about storage and serving needs and plan accordingly. Do you need to store china, flatware, glasses, linens, and serving pieces in the dining room? Will you need a piece that doubles as a server? Have you surveyed your furniture? Do you have an antique or reproduction chest that could add more storage and an extra serving surface? As you plan, remember it's often more interesting to mix, rather than match. In the dining room here, a mahogany dining table and chairs live harmoniously with a built-in sideboard and a china cabinet, both enameled in crisp white.

103 Replicate the detailing from your home in built-in pieces. Notice the china cabinet matches the style and finish of the sideboard.

STORAGE OPTIONS

■ Update a secondhand or vintage sideboard and/or china cabinet with fresh, white enamel paint and new brass pulls.

■ Have a marble top cut for your spiffed-up sideboard. Or, paint or stain the top to contrast with the base and legs.

■ Mix storage pieces in your dining room to create your own look. For example, paint your china cabinet or refinish with a distressed finish and pair with a dark wood sideboard. Add decorative pulls to both pieces.

■ Be playful with periods, too. As long as furniture is in the same scale, contemporary and traditional can grace your space.

104 Counter between your kitchen and dining room? Take advantage of the arrangement (above) with glass shelves mounted with metal supports. Glass keeps the look open and adds display, too. (If you have curved wood shelves, common in homes built in the 1940s and 1950s, replace them with the fresher look of glass.)

105 Have glass shelves cut with rounded, smoothed edges (above) to avoid the dangers of sharp corners. For strength without heavy weight, glass is $\frac{1}{2}$-inch thick.

106 Turn an interior wall of your dining room into a sideboard server with an adjacent wall of floor-to-ceiling cabinets (right). Use the top cabinet to store little-used or seasonal items, such as holiday decorations. This arrangement provides much-needed storage in houses built without basements or attics. It's also safer than garage storage for temperature and humidity control, especially in damp climates.

■ Replace solid doors with glass-paned ones to update an old serving piece. Or, have an old sideboard refinished with a combination of colors or finishes. For subtle variations of color that allow the wood grain to show through, use a translucent glaze or dye.

■ Just replacing pulls on a built-in or freestanding server makes a difference. Look at some of the fun motifs on the market, such as knives and forks or animals. To stretch your dollar, mix these special pulls with plain ones.

■ Combine two metal or sturdy wood wine racks with a glass or painted plywood top for an instant server with storage. Place away from direct sun to avoid damage to your bottles.

107 Incorporate a contemporary-style combination server and china cabinet (left) in a gently arched niche built into your dining room.

108 Stretch your budget by using wood such as pine (left) rather than more costly hardwoods. Finish with a matte, nonyellowing polyurethane to preserve the original color of your storage piece. Use a contrasting color or finish for the decorative top.

109 Space adjustable cabinet shelves to fit serving pieces, such as coffee or tea service (left).

110 Have glass doors fitted as solid pieces without muntin bars (left) for a more contemporary look. Install door pulls at comfortable heights rather than centered on the doors. Or, use touch latches for solid doors.

111 In a small dining room, build a wall of cabinets and open shelves around the window (above). Include a wine rack for handy storage.

112 Find room for a built-in china cabinet (right) by using space between wall studs. This shallow storage works for glasses and plate display.

113 Plan your built-in (above) to incorporate often-untapped space below a window. Use for oversized books, magazines, or photograph albums. Extend the windowsill as a shelf for plants or favorite pottery pieces.

114 Take advantage of a built-in for hanging art (above). When shelves are

symmetrical, center one large, framed painting for a pleasing visual arrangement.

115 Let no window go unnoticed when storage is scarce. Surround with open shelves (right) and tuck a window seat with a hinged top below for often-needed concealed storage. Craft the seat legs for extra detailing.

116 In an open living area, create a dining room library (above) that triples the function and enjoyment of your room.

117 Depending on your wall area, three sections of shelves and cabinets are normally pleasing. This division in threes—called the rule of thirds—often is used to organize design elements. Shelves (above) line up horizontally. This orderly arrangement works well with the traditional tone and furnishings of the room.

118 Include concealed storage adjacent to a dining area. The cabinets (above) hold china, linens, serving pieces, and flatware. Such storage also works well for board games and puzzles and children's art supplies.

119 Need more dining storage? An armoire (above) cupboard adapts with shelving and racks for bar storage. Trays and serving pieces can be accommodated, too.

120 Fit a compact corner cupboard (above left) into a small dining space. Look for vintage pieces or paint or stain an unfinished one for display and storage. Use the top of your piece for extra display.

121 Have fun with a functional built-in serving and storage piece (above center). Choose a motif, here an exaggerated diamond shape, that translates well for cabinet doors and drawers. Use a straightedge to draw your design, then tape off and paint. Trim with details such as the routed pilasters and medallion squares. Seal with a matte finish polyurethane.

122 Adapt storage (above center) to your needs. Silver drawers, lined by an upholsterer with silver cloth, feature a silvercloth flap that wraps over flatware and the larger serving pieces.

123 Make a sideboard server by skirting a plywood base (above right) and having a plywood top cut and shaped to fit. Use a heavy cloth, such as tightly woven linen or cotton, for pleats or gathers. Use space underneath, with baskets, a wicker trunk, or stackable plastic bins or boxes, for extra out-of-sight storage.

STORAGE OPTIONS

■ Hang a small corner cupboard for display in a tiny space. Paint the inside to match or complement your wall color.

■ Stencil a motif or motifs on a painted built-in or freestanding serving piece. Repeat a color from your design for the painted top. Or, stencil a border around the top, too.

■ For a durable serving piece, have a top cut from a salvaged piece of marble or granite. Visit a stone yard to look for bargains.

■ As a contemporary alternative to stone, have the top of a built-in server clad in a neutral or colorful solid-surface material with a decorative edge.

■ Need a sideboard with storage? Look for a vintage or reproduction demi-lune (half round) or other decorative small chest. Line the drawers with silver cloth, to slow tarnish, if you are storing silver pieces.

■ For a make-it-yourself skirted sideboard, buy a pair of stacked, pull-out, vinyl-coated bins on stands and place underneath to organize linens and a varity of serving pieces.

UTILIZE YOUR ENTRY

No square inch of your home is off limits when the storage patrol is on the loose. Convert your home's entry into much more than a pass-through. Tap into its storage potential for keys, packages, umbrellas, and mail that often end up at the front door. Even a basket or a tray on a foyer chest or ledge makes a difference. Use the entry, too, for a carefully organized display that previews your decorating style and collections.

124 Choose furniture that stores with style (left). Here the mirror doubles as a hat rack, and the bench has a drawer for mail and extra keys.

125 Search for unusual ornamental and storage pieces in the scale that fits your entry or foyer. A bamboo cabinet (above) displays pieces from a majolica collection. The majolica umbrella stand holds walking sticks.

126 Measure your entry carefully when choosing a piece of freestanding furniture. The depth is as important as the height and width to avoid blocking the front door.

127 Look for the simplest solution. You can't go wrong with a vintage wooden trunk (right) to store handy items in the entry. Use baskets or boxes inside the trunk to aid your organizing.

128 Add a box on top of a trunk or a small chest and make that your one-stop drop for the necessities—keys, wallet, and checkbook—that help you get out of the house every day.

129 *Find multiple solutions for your front door storage needs (left). A vintage oak basket on a stand for mail and packages, and an umbrella rack help the family stay organized.*

130 *Designate a storage piece in an adjacent room (left). If a chest or narrow secretary won't fit in your entry, find space in another convenient spot.*

131 *When space is extremely limited, install a narrow decorative shelf on brackets as the place for mail and keys. Paint the shelf to match the trim color for an accent. Or, as a quick solution, have a glass shelf cut with beveled edges and install it on decorative metal brackets.*

132 *If you need a place to pull off boots as well as drop packages, build a bench at the front entry (above). Space below could work for baskets.*

SEATING WITH STORAGE

Double the usefulness of a window seat with hidden storage. Whether your home has an alcove, a bay, a stair landing, or just an empty spot by a pair of windows, there's room for a seat. Hinged tops, often in sections, are easy to install and access. However, if you plan window seat storage in a child's room or playroom, use safer sliding doors or open base storage to avoid pinching fingers.

133 In the dining room (right), use baskets inside a window seat to organize table linens or extra serving pieces. If space is tight, store china, flatware, and glassware.

134 Conceal hinged storage access with a decorative padded seat cushion (right) or cushions. Or, for books and magazines, consider accessible open storage.

135 Beyond the window seat, this compact dining room maximizes space with painted shelves for houseplants (right). Hang shelves at two levels.

■ Place a sturdy, open bench at your window. Add a cushion for comfort and use the space below for baskets or boxes. A flat-top trunk is another option for concealed storage.

■ To create storage with a garden look, arrange a rustic wood or metal bench below a window to show off plants and garden objects. Fill baskets below with gardening books, tools, and accessories.

■ Flank a window with matching freestanding bookcases and place a low bench or trunk, painted to match, underneath. You'll emulate the look of built-ins without construction.

136 In a room where the view is paramount, frame a window seat with floor-to-ceiling windows (above). Where space allows, repeat the style of the construction in cabinets. Here the cabinets with open shelving enrich the storage.

137 What's better than reading in a cozy nook? When space allows, incorporate bookshelves (right) in an alcove planned for a window seat.

138 Work in storage to the max. Bookshelves (right) flank both sides of the built-in.

INSTANT STYLE
FOR EVERY BUDGET

Sometimes you want storage right now. And you need more than one or two ideas. You require a whole room full of ways to store, organize, and display. When you don't have time for built-ins or if you want less-than-permanent solutions, look to retail sources for ideas and inspiration. From stores and catalogs that specialize in storage and home decorating to the large home centers and discount stores, you'll find products in every style and for every budget. Think, too, about import stores, secondhand shops, thrift stores, and flea markets. With a little imagination, you can find storage uses from an array of practical and decorative objects. Remember, too, that well-chosen products have multiple uses. When you find easy answers, you'll have decorating elements that work in a variety of other settings.

139 *Convert tea-table-height wicker baskets, (opposite) into cocktail tables, perfect storage for throws or newspapers. The handsome metal side table is also a container, and the striped wood photo frame stores tiny, easy-to-misplace objects.*

140 *Invest in one focal-point piece (left). This funky cabinet combines both utilitarian and decorative storage.*

141 *What is more versatile than an imported basket (above right) that gathers magazines, newspapers, and books with style. Choose a sturdier version to keep firewood handy by your hearth.*

142 *Give a versatile canvas-lined wicker basket (right) a new role for bread or party snacks. Team it with a chrome-plated steel wine caddy for a lighthearted party look.*

STORAGE, THE KEY ELEMENT OF KITCHEN design, imparts style and function to kitchens large or small. When you think of how a kitchen looks, works, and lives, you are evaluating how well the storage performs. At its best, storage saves steps and eliminates frustrating searches for necessary kitchen tools and gadgets. Well-planned cabinets, drawers, and shelves maximize space, freeing up corners or counters for the display, dining, and seating options we all want today. And storage moves out of the confines of the kitchen into

KITCHENS
AND SERVICE AREAS

hardworking laundries, pantries, and entryways. Whether you're building, remodeling, or enhancing with quick solutions found in retail stores, in this chapter you'll find practical ideas for busy kitchens.

Incorporate open shelves in the range hood over an island cooktop. Used for a collection of tea pots, the shelves translate utilitarian storage into a striking focal point for safe display. Drawers at the bar keep linens and silverware at hand.

STORE
WITH STYLE

As kitchens become our family living and dining rooms, storage reflects style as much as practicality. Cabinets are treated as fine furniture that adds to the value and enjoyment of this room. If you are remodeling or building, you have the option of custom, semi-custom, or stock cabinets. Designed by architects, kitchen designers, or cabinetmakers, custom cabinets can be tailored to fit odd spaces and allow choices of design, wood, and finish, plus personalized storage options.

Semi-custom cabinets are modified from stock designs to fit your needs. The British and European cabinets sold through dealers are semi-custom. Stock cabinets, from home centers and dealers, offer ever-increasing choices of prices, designs, configurations, finishes, and storage options.

STORAGE OPTIONS

■ *Visit a discount store or home center to find easy ways to customize your kitchen storage. Add items such as lazy Susans to make inaccessible corners easy to reach and use.*

■ *Use products such as racks for glasses and hooks for cups to maximize every bit of cabinet space.*

■ *No pantry? Add shelves at the back of the kitchen door to store canned goods and seasonal items.*

143 *Pull-out cabinets (below left) with vinyl-coated racks. Make kitchen recycling part of the everyday routine. A standard base cabinet is normally sized to hold two kitchen bins—an easy way to divide glass from plastic. Home centers, discount stores, and shops specializing in home organizing offer a wide selection of products to aid your family's recycling efforts.*

144 *Designed as built-in furniture (above), this compact pantry keeps staples handy without taking up the space of a walk-in pantry. Drawers below add storage for pots, pans, and miscellaneous items.*

145 *Take advantage of the space under a cooktop (left) for drawers for pots and pans. Kitchen designers and architects often recommend deep drawers, rather than open cabinets, to improve organization.*

146 *When you build a desk into the kitchen (opposite), add drawers for files.*

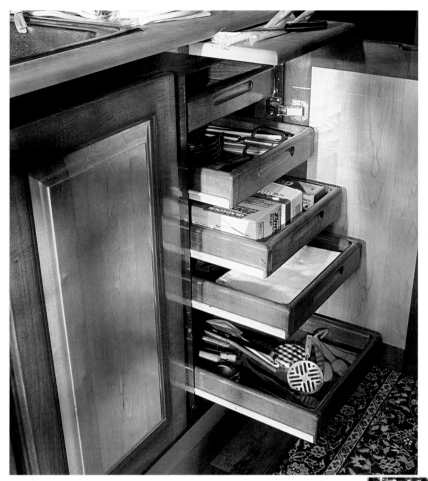

■ To revitalize existing cabinets, paint the frame and doors in contrasting colors. If you are dealing with stained rather than painted cabinets, sand and apply a commercial deglazer so the paint will adhere. Also consider replacing some solid doors with glass-panel cabinet doors.

■ Mix colors and finishes of base and wall cabinets and add decorative pulls.

■ Retrofit existing base cabinets for more organized storage with pull-out bins, racks, or lazy Susans for tight corners. Or, use baskets or color-coded plastic trays if you need to store easy-to-lose items.

■ No time for custom? Buy a decorative shelf for spices. For fun, paint the shelf in a contrasting accent color.

147 When remodeling a kitchen, adjust counter heights (left) to existing windows. Use space below for a lower storage cabinet, here between the sink and window. Even the window sill contributes as a ledge for sun-loving plants.

148 As another space-saver in a compact kitchen, vary the heights of wall cabinets (left) to make room for special items. The over-the-sink lighting is mounted under the center cabinet while the wall space works for the always-needed paper-towel holder. Even the knives find storage with grooves in the butcher-block backsplash.

149 Make every inch work in a small kitchen. Add extras such as the pull-out cutting board (left) and the rack for dish towels to keep necessities close at hand.

150 Have trouble finding small kitchen tools and gadgets? Or keeping up with sandwich bags? Instead of shelves or deep drawers, add shallow drawers (above) to keep what you need always within view and easy reach. Adjust the spacing to meet your needs.

151 If you frequently use heavy kitchen equipment, such as the mixer (right) or a food processor, consider storing it on its own pull-out and pull-up tray. Check with kitchen designers, custom kitchen dealers, or cabinetmakers for sources and installation.

152 One narrow shelf (right) can make a huge difference in storing your spices and seasonings. Hanging it near, but not over the stove, is ideal as heat affects taste and freshness.

153 Take advantage of an open plan to create a storage-oriented peninsula (left) or a freestanding island. To make the most of your storage options, include drawers, cabinets for large items, and open display shelves. Transform a work/storage piece into a design focal point with decorative columns on the corners.

154 Be imaginative with open storage (left). Instead of a standard pot rack or wall-mounted plate rack, have a cabinetmaker build a special piece, such as this eye-catching pot rack constructed with dowels and shelving. Cables attach it to the ceiling for stability.

155 Who needs cabinet doors? For the ultimate in accessible storage (below), use open wall and under-the-counter storage in place of conventional cabinets. Vary the heights of the shelves or install adjustable shelves to expand your options. Here, 5-inch-deep shelves display canning jars within easy view and reach.

156 Include personal touches, such as wine racks (below), that make your kitchen work well for you. And take advantage of every bit of space—here over the built-in refrigerator—for extra decorative display or storage.

STORAGE OPTIONS

■ No island? Need temporary storage that can move with you? Buy a butcher-block cart on wheels from a specialty home design catalog, kitchen shop, or import store. Some larger home centers or discount stores have similar items. The carts are built with storage such as wine racks. Or, substitute a work table for a rustic solution.

■ If concealed storage isn't an overwhelming need, replace a section of wall-mounted cabinets with open shelves for canning jars and decorative plates or glasses.

■ Replace a section of base cabinets for open shelves with sturdy, decorative baskets for produce and kitchen linens.

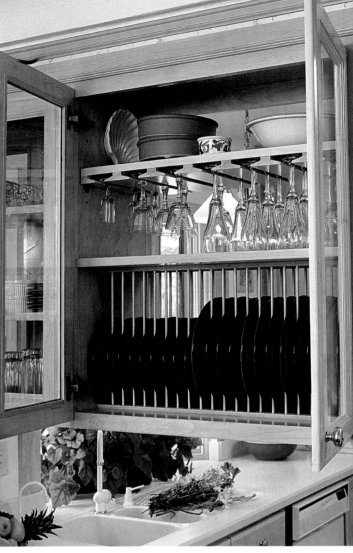

157 *Fit stock cabinets (above left) with easy-glide drawers and wood dividers sized to your china collection. Or put stock plastic or wire dividers into drawers for an instant solution. If you use part of such a unit for bar storage, reinforce the drawers for the weight of liquor bottles.*

158 *Who wants to iron and re-iron tablecloths and linens? Keep yours neat with a pull-out unit (left) constructed with oversized wooden dowels mounted inside a frame. Use similar storage for oversized napkins and linen or cotton luncheon place mats.*

159 *Adapt storage to your specific needs (above). Have an upper shelf custom-made for stemware storage or install tracks on the underside of any shelf. Use dowels to adapt for vertical plate storage inside a glass-front cabinet. These cabinets often are open on both sides for quick and easy access.*

160 *Construct your own butler's pantry (right) by building shelving around a window in a back hall or laundry room.*

161 *Choose adjustable shelves (right) to vary the heights. Note the mix of plywood and glass shelves in this unit.*

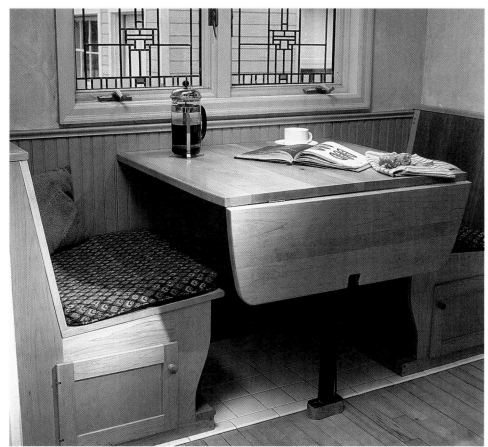

162 *Build in your breakfast table, cafe booth style (left) to save space in the kitchen. Use hinged doors for access to under-the-seat storage. A fold-down, hinged seat top adds more space savings, too.*

163 *As an alternative, build a window seat or banquette with concealed storage. Space under the seat houses often-awkward items, such as telephone books, or current magazines and miscellaneous items. For a quick solution, use hinged-seat benches, with or without backs, or a farm table with drawers.*

164 *When you want storage close at hand, try banquette seating with open shelves (above). Here two shelves fit snugly under the seat. To store a basket or books vertically, choose one shelf in this space.*

OPEN TO NEW IDEAS

Kitchens that are part of family living space demand decorative and storage functions. When you live and entertain as well as work in the kitchen, you'll enjoy the space when you accessorize with the collectibles you love. If you are building or remodeling, include open, display storage. Or, if you are simply freshening up your kitchen, hang decorative shelve for pretty display.

165 When you collect, incorporate your finds into storage planning (right). Here, a collector designed country-style cabinets with open—and safe—display for breakables. Glass fronts on open cabinets provide additional protection.

166 As alternatives, mix glass-front and solid cabinets in the same kitchen. Or, use the tops of cabinets for instant and easy display.

167 Even a small island with a cooktop (right) yields decorative storage. Use one or both ends for shelves for collectibles, plates, and smaller books or cookbooks.

■**STORAGE OPTIONS**

■ *Purchase a new or vintage hanging cabinet or corner cupboard for open storage in your kitchen. If an old piece has a worn finish, simply clean it and enjoy the timeworn patina.*

■ *Buy ready-made picture ledges, available from decorating shops and specialty catalogs, and have a frame shop rout grooves for plates. Hang them around your kitchen as plate racks.*

■ *Hang three ready-made decorative shelves in graduated sizes on a blank wall. Paint in different colors for accents.*

■ *Find new uses for standard objects. Stools, benches, and painted bookcases are ideal for instant storage display. Or, place a narrow table against the wall and arrange baskets underneath for more storage.*

168 If walls and counters don't provide enough space for cabinet storage (above), mount a unit from the ceiling over an island or peninsula. For light and accessibility, design the unit so glass doors open on both sides.

169 Make every inch count with a window seat with drawers and deep cookbook shelves (above) under the island.

170 Create accessible storage with open, curved shelving (right). No hard-to-reach corners here, and everything, from pottery to oversized books, is in full view. Mix in glass doors and drawer accents for style and design interest.

STORAGE OPTIONS

■ Use as much wall space as you can when kitchen storage is limited. Install a plate rack and use it for dishes and saucers.

■ In a country- or cottage-style kitchen, add Shaker pegs for kitchen tools and gadgets. Or, substitute an expandable, wall-mounted hat rack for tool or basket storage. Hang mesh bags from racks to store produce such as onions. Also, hang Shaker pegs or a hat rack at the kitchen door for shopping bags.

■ Translate ideas for handy tool storage such as perforated hardboard for kitchen tools. Use S-hooks for hanging.

■ Hang a basket or two from your pot rack for kitchen linens, such as towels and napkins.

171 Design an island or peninsula (above) with a pair of flanking open shelves sized for cookbooks. Choose adjustable shelves for versatility.

172 For a sleek look that allows stored items to become part of the decor, replace solid cabinet doors with glass (above). Or, order new cabinets with this mix of glass and solid. Inside, vary the shelf heights to hold a variety of objects in different heights.

173 Create symmetry in a contemporary kitchen (above) with to-the-ceiling cabinets over the refrigerator and wall oven. Save for seasonal or infrequently used items, such as punch bowls.

174 Even in a kitchen with open shelves or glass cabinet doors, reserve at least one section for concealed storage. Depending on accessibility needs, use wall-mounted or base cabinets.

175 Tailor storage to your needs. The pull-out drawer (right) provides a marble surface for pastry making or kneading bread. Keep related supplies and implements nearby.

176 Take advantage of the ceiling to hang one or more pot racks (right). Use S-hooks to expand storage. In some areas, local blacksmiths make these custom pieces.

177 In a tiny kitchen (left), keep storage as open as possible. The shelf below the cookware holds canisters and spices.

178 If space allows in a small kitchen, hang multiple shelves. Use the hard-to-reach top shelves for little-used items. Add fruit baskets or colorful plastic bins to organize storage. Or, use Shaker pegs to hang kitchen tools and gadgets such as turners and spoons.

179 When space is very tight (left), bolt iron pot racks to the wall from floor to ceiling as shown. Use S-hooks for simple organization. These racks are sold in specialty home catalogs, kitchen shops, and home centers.

180 Be neat when you use your walls for storage and display. As you buy pots and pans, collect only one or two types and hang them together as shown (left). Here, the graduated sizes add interest.

181 Turn a blank wall into a decorative asset (above). Add a shelf with decorative brackets for kitchen collectibles. Use hooks and nails to hang pot holders and decorative molds below.

182 In a country-style kitchen, use the back of your range for storage (above). Remove objects that are susceptible to heat damage.

183 Think beyond cabinets and drawers when you plan storage. When space is tight and you need more work, dining, or serving areas, ask a cabinetmaker to design a pull-out table (right). This extension table has three leaves that unfold from a drawerlike panel; legs pull down for a quick counter.

184 Plan storage to blend with the style and era of your home (right). Here the owners of a 1930s vintage home gave stock cabinets a period look with curved end panels and open shelves. The waffle-textured glass in the door fits with the era while providing a degree of concealed storage for necessities.

185 If you have room, plan a second storage area, such as the open shelves (right) for extra decorative and practical storage options.

186 Include matching baskets with handles (right) for concealed storage for nonperishable vegetables or other kitchen supplies.

187 Add decorative elements (lower right) to elevate utilitarian storage to high style. Below the counter, the gentle arches and baluster supports impart the look of fine furniture to a useful storage piece.

188 Use large decorative jars (lower right) to hold bulk quantities of food. Be sure the interior finishes are safe for food.

AND A SPACE FOR EVERYTHING

Utilitarian spaces—like laundry areas and mudrooms—require maximum storage in a minimum of square footage. This laundry/hobby/bar space uses every precious inch. High-functioning spaces like this don't just happen; evaluation, measuring, and planning ensure success. If you are remodeling or building, allow room for storage and organizing centers. Depending on your floor plan and family needs, locate these areas near the back door, family entrance, or kitchen. Or, if your laundry is in the basement, or as is common in some newer plans, near the bedrooms, consider expanding it to serve other functions.

■ STORAGE OPTIONS

■ **Prop up serving trays under cabinets for instant artwork that can be moved when more counter space is needed.**

■ **In open areas, keep the sundries out of sight. Hide the washer and dryer behind a partition wall with the more visually pleasing work table in plain view.**

189 In a small, multipurpose space, coordinate cabinetry (opposite) for a unified look throughout.

190 Slots under the cabinet neatly hold oversize serving platters, cookie sheets, or other flat items (opposite).

191 Laundry supplies are necessary but rather unglamorous. Stowed behind cabinets over the washer and under the sink (above), these items are at hand but out of sight.

192 Think display as well as storage. The arched shallow cabinet directly over the sink (upper right) keeps glassware in view right where it's needed. Slots on the underside of the middle shelf hold pub-style glass storage. Deeper, taller cabinets on either side display bigger serving pieces.

193 Keep hobby spaces inspirational and functional. Ideas as well as reminders deserve space on the bulletin board (lower right).

ORGANIZE YOUR LAUNDRY

We all have to do it—that daily or weekly chore that ensures clean clothes and linens for the family. To get the most out of this space, combine it with other needs. Do you need a place to arrange flowers, pot plants, or start seeds? A sink for hand washables is handy for the double-duty potting area, too. Or, what about a gift-wrapping center? Or a home sewing center that shares the ironing board and folding table? And don't forget the original purpose of the laundry room. Just a few simple changes add labor- and clothes-savings convenience. Consider racks for socks or hose, a flat surface to dry knits and sweaters, and color-coded bins to separate light and dark clothes.

194 Just as nature intended, take advantage of all the natural light available. Shelves (right) add layers for pots, using the full level of light.

195 For a thriving planting area, water is just as important as light. A deep sink is also a great place to pot and water plants (right). Dirt and water overflows stay confined for quick and easy clean-up.

196 Plant lovers can never have too much dirt. A large, open, floor-level space makes a home for a full-size plastic garbage container (right) to hold gallons of fresh earth. Adjacent open shelves hold items grouped by height and weight. Heavy stacks of terra-cotta pots slide out as needed along the floor.

197 Height has advantages, especially when you need space for two hobbies. Even in a snug corner of the laundry room (upper left), there's plenty of room to dry flowers on a rack overhead while finely detailed fly-fishing lures are crafted on the work surface. Drawers, cabinets, and open shelves are sized and assigned for materials.

198 Laundry rooms are notorious for falling victim to chaos, and the likelihood of the freshly washed falling in with the yet-to-be-laundered is significant. Not here: Freshly laundered shirts (right) stay neat hung up top, right out of the dryer.

199 Four individual laundry baskets (right), with their own cubbyholes, presort loads—ready to head right for the washing machine. Make sure you have plenty of continuous counter space so clean laundry can be sorted and folded.

200 A gift wrapping center (left) organizes paper, boxes, and bows. Stash gifts bought in advance here, too.

201 Pull-out cabinets (left) make excellent use of storage space in laundry rooms. Craft supplies, cleaning essentials, and garden tools fit neatly in this stowaway space.

202 Use the space over the washer and dryer for a bar to air-dry small items (right). Add a shelf to keep soap and sundries at hand. Even a small shelf that bridges the gap between machines can keep items from slipping out of sight.

THE MESS STOPS HERE

Think how neat your home could be if the family left the clutter of everyday life at the back door instead of strewing it through the family room and depositing it on the stairs. Think of the time you would save in the mornings if daily necessities—from jackets and umbrellas to backpacks and sporting gear—were in one organized, orderly place. Assess the space your family really uses and consider what needs to be there. Remember, items can be changed seasonally.

■ *Keep only in-season coats, scarves, and hats near the door. Too many coats hanging on pegs create chaos and lead to items piling up on the floor.*

■ *Always leave a peg or two open for extra items. In busy households, make sure everyone has a peg or two specifically for his or her things, especially if one family member is a drop-and-run specialist. Then the coat dropping culprit will have no excuse.*

■ *Shop for coat storage as you would for room furnishings. Creating a pleasant place encourages neatness, especially if your open-air closet is by the front door.*

■ *Make room for seating. If it's just a stool, providing a place to take off muddy shoes confines tracked-in dirt to the doorway.*

■ *Tiny hooks or a low shelf next to a peg rack can line up keys or catch sunglasses as folks come and go.*

203 Pegs are perfect for just-in-the-door storage (left). Coats, hats, athletic equipment, even the dog's leash can share space and be ready for the next use. Two levels of pegs double the available amount of storage; less-used items stowed on the lower level will be covered by frequently-used items on the top row. An extra peg on the side wall makes sure a special item is always within reach and sight.

204 A bench with drawers (left) keeps the look neat and avoids the mad scramble when everyone is rushing out to work, school, or practice. Shoes and boots at the back of the bench leave room for sitting down in front. Out-of-season hats, scarves, gloves, and athletic equipment take up residence in the drawers.

205 When coat closets are full, make room for accessories in the hall (above). Simple pegs hold hats, gloves, and scarves. A shelf above makes room for display. A narrow bench provides a place to change shoes—whether you're coming or going.

206 Hallway traffic is aided by a row of Shaker pegs (right), and outerwear can be grabbed on the way out or quickly hung up on the way in. Folded umbrellas or walking sticks use the space below efficiently.

207 Plan your family entrance for your children's interests. And if they play multiple sports through the year, design accordingly (above). Here, the family entrance is a mini locker room with a built-in unit for sports gear and equipment.

208 Measure the sizes of key pieces of equipment such as tennis rackets, baseball bats, and hockey sticks (above) and build shelving and bins to size.

209 Also, allow space for muddy or dirty athletic shoes and jackets to dry (above). If space permits, designate sections of the built-in for individual shelves or bins for each child. A bulletin board is a convenient way to keep game and practice times on the family calendar.

210 Have at least one accessible bin (lower center) to store large or oddly shaped items. The door swings out on a chain to make it easy to search for just the right practice bat or bow or tennis racket or lacrosse stick. Measure the height of the tallest item you think you'll store and then add extra inches to make sure this all-in-one bin will work for a variety of sports equipment.

211 If your children need a place to pull off snow or rain boots or change from in-line skates, add a built-in seating with handy sports storage (upper and lower right). With such a simple plywood addition, they'll have a place to stash outdoor toys and gear and even wait for a ride to school. Because hinged tops can pinch little fingers, wait until your children are out of the toddler stage to add this to your toy storage options. Apply a tough enamel paint to stand up to the inevitable scratches and scrapes of everyday life.

Stylish Storables
TO KEEP IN SIGHT

As our kitchens evolve into family living, dining, and entertaining centers, storage ideas expand beyond the utilitarian to the creative and innovative. Think of what you need to store and where you need to store it. If storage items are visible, consider how you can go beyond the utilitarian to add visual interest and style. Look for ways to use different items, such as pottery, glassware, and baskets, that appeal to you and still meet your storage needs. Instead of standard kitchen canisters, for example, visit an import store and look at the array of glass and pottery. Or, even more fun, shop at crafts fairs or flea markets to find items that can be converted into practical new uses.

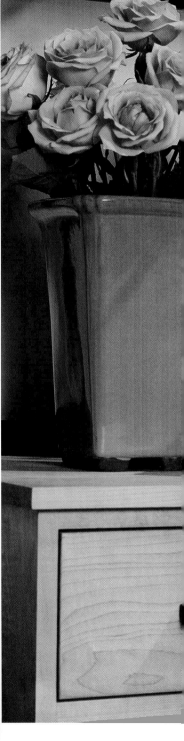

212 Stowed beneath the buffet, candles, napkin rings, and linens are organized in canvas-clad wicker baskets (left). Grouping a set of similar baskets in a variety of sizes allows you to cluster miscellaneous items on open shelves without having a jumble of containers.

213 Decorative baskets corral unruly items into place. A chrome-plated steel basket with handles (below) keeps fresh fruit neatly arranged, and a simple wire basket with wood handles holds towels in a tidy formation.

214 A variety of takes on the old-fashioned pie carrier (below) offers excellent multitier plate storage. Baskets with several compartments transport flatware and table linens to the table or buffet with ease. You needn't even unload these carriers; they serve as gracefully as they store.

215 The classic ginger jar (above) is a beautiful home for fresh-baked cookies. The elegant shape is echoed in the glass apothecary jars with shapely cast-iron lids. Use them for herbs, especially those with color, to add pizzazz to kitchen counters—just be sure you choose lead-free jars intended to store food safely.

216 A vintage maple syrup can, dressed up with a cloth napkin (below), becomes a colorful catchall for cooking utensils. Scope out secondhand shops for bargains.

CLOTHES, LINENS, TOWELS, BOOKS. The storage needs in our beds and baths are great and small. Whether your space is generous or cramped, start with the basics. If you are building or remodeling, look through this chapter for ways to get the most of closets and built-ins for both hanging and stacked items plus ideas to use every bit of a bath for clever, attractive storage. Or, if you are working with existing closets, chests, or dressers, you'll find ways to maximize the storage opportunities with simple remodelings, adap-

BEDROOMS
AND BATHS

tations of vintage chests and cabinets, and storage organizers. Baths, too, benefit from the array of organizing items on the market. For easy-to-accomplish, affordable fun ideas, see Quick Fixes on pages 100-101.

For his own organized master retreat (opposite), Minneapolis architect Geoff Warner designed storage that's accessible by a system of slatted doors, operated by weights and pulleys. Turn to page 86 for more on the room, with storage revealed.

SUITE OF MASTERFUL IDEAS

Small spaces in old houses call for creative solutions, especially if you are a young, on-a-budget architect who lives and works in the same vintage bungalow. With the downstairs bedrooms allocated to his office, Geoff Warner literally had to move up for a master suite and study. And with a baby on the way to share the converted attic, he and his wife were even more conscious of space planning. As a solution, Warner combined stock plywood, recycled packing-crate wood, and clever engineering for the storage units here and on page 85. Mounted on galvanized steel tracks, four plank doors are balanced by a system of pulleys and counterweights that allows them to pull down easily or push up for access to the closet and television. Warner used the remaining recycled wood for a freestanding, space-dividing storage unit that serves both the master bedroom and the adjacent nursery.

217 When space is tight, choose perforated clothes hampers (above) that are too handsome to hide.

218 Take advantage of knee wall space in an attic-to-bedroom conversion to build in storage such as these plywood chests (above). Use a lower chest under hanging clothes.

219 Construct rustic storage from packing crates (right) or other recycled wood. Include open shelves for display of family photographs.

STORAGE OPTIONS

■ *In an attic bedroom, use narrow bi-fold doors to conceal under-the-eaves closets. Or, as an instant solution, simply hang racks for clothes and conceal with a vintage screen or shutters.*
■ *In an old-fashioned bedroom, use white wicker hampers, instead of metal canisters, before clothes go to the laundry or cleaners.*
■ *Instead of building in chests or drawers, look for small, unfinished pieces that can be painted or stained. Or use a wicker basket with a top for closet storage under hanging clothes.*
■ *For safety, use acrylic or plastic containers for cotton balls and swabs in children's baths.*

220 In a small bath, incorporate shelves around and under the window frames (above). Use small shelves under the medicine cabinet.

221 Add shelving units (above) when space is too tight for a storage closet. Curves are safer than sharp angles in such tight spaces.

222 When storage is in view (above), find attractive containers or glass jars for the essentials, such as cotton balls.

223 Even a changing table with drawers and open shelves can be built in when space is limited (right).

224 Plan units so they can be adapted as baby grows. Here the middle drawer (right) is easily removed so the unit can be converted to a desk with storage when the space is no longer a nursery.

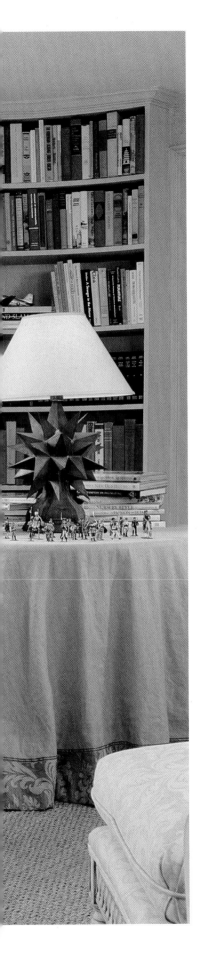

MAKE ROOM TO READ

If your den or family room is the hub of busy family life, turn your bedroom into the ultimate pleasure for a book lover—a quiet library with handsome and generous storage for your beloved volumes. Plan your space—no matter the size—with at least one wall of floor-to-ceiling built-ins. Adjustable shelves allow you to vary heights for tall art books or small paperbacks. This initial investment will give you the pleasure of having space to organize your books and mix in collections or family photographs. If you prefer flexibility, have a carpenter build stackable freestanding units that can move to another home. Or, buy two or three tall bookcases and arrange them as your book wall.

226 Take advantage of the potential of bedroom walls with floor-to-ceiling built-in bookshelves (opposite).

227 Box in windows with shelves above and window seats (opposite) to use every bit of space for storage and display.

228 Be creative with specialized storage. Add a trio of woven boxes from an import store (opposite) to store clutter such as papers or magazines, or to keep items such as family photographs or needlework neat and convenient.

229 Use the space under a skirted table for stacked boxes or bins to store what you need but not necessarily what you want in view. Some plywood bases are made with a shelf that's ideal to stack magazines. As another option, stash storage baskets under the fabric folds.

225 Remember the most classic storage of all—the desk. Choose one with the drawer space you need (above). Even a writing table works if you only need storage for supplies.

ELEMENTS OF MOBILITY

When clutter consumes your bedroom, take the easy way out and go shopping. The stylish organizers here were gleaned from a few hours of cruising through an import store and a specialty organizing shop. Home centers and discount stores as well as decorating and gift shops are also good sources. If you like catalog shopping, see the sources on page 112. And think past intended uses. The fun of stylish storage is looking for new uses for your favorite finds.

230 Stack decorative matching boxes (above) *in graduated sizes to keep items such as earrings, costume jewelry, socks, tights, hose, or scarves handy for the morning rush.*

231 Make the most of *your bedside storage with an accent box on a stand (right) from an import store. Decorative hinged boxes are easy to access and handy for tissues, glasses, reading materials, and miscellaneous clutter.*

232 Shop around for an
interesting dresser, such as this
burnished metal one (above),
or a dressing table with drawers
from the '30s or '40s.
Secondhand furniture stores and
thrift shops are great places to
shop for unusual pieces.

233 Tired of dresser-top
clutter? Look for colorful boxes
in varying shapes, sizes, and
materials (above) to hold small
pieces of jewelry.

234 Create instant and
affordable dresser-top storage
with an enameled serving tray
(above) from a gift shop or
import store. Or, substitute a
flat basket for a tropics-inspired
accent.

235 Organize closet
shelves with creative solutions
such as these reproductions of
classic hatboxes (upper right).
Or, look for thrift store boxes
or small suitcases or hat boxes.

236 Take advantage of
closet organizers, such as this
rack (upper right), available
at specialty shops, home centers,
and discount stores.

237 Keep order with
specialty items, such as this
hanging rack designed for folded
sweaters or knits (right).

238 Add ready-made,
vinyl-coated shelving units (right)
to a standard closet to keep
linens and extra pillows handy.

OPEN & SHUT OPTIONS

Sometimes you want storage open and part of your room's design; sometimes you want storage discreetly hidden from public view. For the most pleasing results, adapt to the room setting and to what you are storing or displaying. When your needs call for more elaborate solutions, such as the panels or Oriental-style screens shown here, consult with an architect or interior designer. A few hours of consultation can yield ideas and sketches that a carpenter or cabinetmaker can translate into your ideal storage.

239 *Conceal storage stylishly with shelves behind lacquered, dense particleboard doors (above). Hidden pivot hinges allow the panels to open with a light touch for easy access to stacked linens and towels.*

240 *Plan an all-in-one bedroom built-in (right) to combine a chest for clothes, bookshelves, and storage for the television, electronic equipment, and tapes. Vary the depths of drawers and paint and detail the drawer fronts for colorful accents. Design with adjustable shelves for flexibility.*

241 *Space too precious for a closet door? Hang a contrast-lined and piped drapery panel (right) instead for quick access and a stylish design accent. This panel hides shallow shelves and a shoe rack.*

■ *Replace sliding closet doors on tracts, often found in houses built in the 1940s and 1950s, with easier-to-access bifold doors. Paint the doors to match trim.*

■ *Hang narrow floor-to-ceiling shelves or picture ledges in a blank hallway. Narrow ledges are a fun way to display family photographs.*

■ *If storage necessities are spilling out of your closets, buy a clothes rack and angle it in your bedroom corner behind a pretty freestanding screen.*

■ *If your bedroom closet is generously sized, buy a cart for your portable television. Save floor space by rolling it out only when you want to watch it.*

242 Turn simple, utilitarian shelves into a design accent (above). In a dressing nook off the master bedroom, floor-to-ceiling shelves built for hats are as attractive as they are useful. The neatness and space show off each hat to its best advantage.

243 Stay focused when storage doubles as display (above). Use decorative hatboxes or other interesting boxes to hide small items or inevitable clutter. (Smaller items will be easier to find in boxes, too.)

244 Emulate the inventive Orient with sliding, Shoji-screen-style doors (right). This 19-foot-long wall of accessible storage conceals the necessities of the master bedroom, including the television.

245 Build your sliding screens (right) to the ceiling and use the harder-to-reach spaces for out-of-season clothing, luggage, or rarely used seasonal items. Include drawers and open spaces for shoes as shown.

STORAGE OPTIONS

■ Maximize storage for every closet, no matter what size. Double hang racks for shirts, slacks, blouses, and suits. Use in children's closets, too.

■ Attach pegs, hooks, or racks to the insides of closet doors for extra storage for hats, ties, scarves, and chains.

■ Use the backs of closet doors for racks or cloth pouches for shoes and small items.

■ If you can't add a double rack and need more storage, utilize the space under shirts or blouses with a low chest or a wicker hamper for out-of-season clothes.

■ Add clear plastic bins in a child's closet to keep clutter and toys at bay but easy to find.

246 Building or adding a master suite? Design a combination dressing room and walk-in closet (above). Open shelves, racks, bins, pegs, and hooks create the ultimate in organized storage.

247 Plan storage according to your needs and clothes. Hats are easy to crush, for example, so allow shelf or hanging space (above). Racks for belts, scarves, and jewelry keep accessories convenient.

248 Include a cube of drawers (left) for folded clothes. The 36-inch-high top is convenient as a counter for packing.

249 Plan a room-dividing storage unit (right) between your bed and dressing area or bath. Use bed-flanking shelves to keep reading glasses and books handy, and use the sides for bookshelves.

250 For master suite luxury, add a mini kitchen with storage behind closed doors (above). Flank with open, conventional, floor-to-ceiling bookshelves.

251 Stock the cabinets for concealed storage for coffee mugs, supplies, glasses, plates, silverware, and snacks. Use for extra storage as needed.

252 Literally think inside the box to add storage to a traditional style bedroom furnished with antiques (left). Shaker boxes in graduated sizes or a wicker or wooden box enhance the look while hiding necessities and clutter. And you can't go wrong with an antique wood trunk for blankets, pillows, out-of-season clothing, or extra reading material.

UTILIZE YOUR BATH

Large or small, shared or a private retreat, every bath promises storage options. For a master or shared family bath, look for ways to work in all the essentials of towels and shampoos, soaps, and grooming supplies. If you have a hall closet nearby, relieve some of the storage burden by using it for extra towels and supplies. But if everything must fit in the

253 Use a wall of storage cabinets (above) as a room divider between the bath and master bedroom. The routing detail and pulls give these doors a contemporary look; shelves are adjustable.

254 Allow space for an open cube (above) as a focal-point display for a favorite object, plant, or seasonal flowers. This also lets in light, another plus.

255 Work with a finish carpenter or cabinetmaker to build a sink vanity (above) that emulates the look of vintage furniture. Incorporate period detailing, such as beaded-board doors.

256 Size drawers under the sink (above) to fit your needs and add organizing convenience. Use drawer dividers to keep items neat and handy.

bath, look for ways to get the most storage in what is often limited space. When you build or remodel, design floor-to-ceiling storage, perhaps on one side of the sink, or under-the-sink cabinets. Or, if you are dealing with an existing space, even small extras, such as a shelf or two or a hanging wall cabinet, make a difference in how your bath works. Take advantage of extra floor space, too, by adding a small baker's rack, bench, plant stand, or an interesting accent chair as a place to stack towels and washcloths. And don't forget wall space for hooks and racks for towels and robes. Use the back of the door, for example, for extra towel racks, and remember to hang racks, pegs, and hooks at reachable heights for young children. A child-height toothbrush rack is another help for an organized bath.

257 Recycle a vintage cabinet (above) for charming storage. Paint to match your trim and decor.

258 Skirt an old-fashioned sink (above) and use the concealed space for baskets or flat plastic boxes. (Don't use for cleaning supplies or anything that could be dangerous if you have young children.)

259 Free up bedroom or closet space by having drawers built into a bathroom wall for a dressing area (right). Use smaller drawers for socks and hose.

260 Waste no space; have upper cabinets (right) built for extra storage, such as out-of-season coverlets or spare towels.

■ *Want to convert a chest or sideboard into a vanity? Have a marble or granite top cut to fit as shown at left. Or, start with a self-rimming sink to keep water off the original wood top.*

■ *To be sure your project will work in an existing bath, consult with a plumber and a skilled carpenter. The top drawers of a chest may have to be reshaped if you want to retain them for storage.*

■ *Choose a piece that fits your bath. Look for a small chest, such as a French style demi-lune (half round) for a tiny powder room. Waterproof natural wood with polyurethane; seal a painted piece with high-gloss acrylic.*

261 *Convert a vintage chest, sideboard, or cabinet into a stylish vanity (above). Match the wood for a shelf or two.*

262 *Add a small patio or outdoor table (above) for plants and extra towels. Use small boxes for extra storage options.*

263 *In an old-fashioned bath long on charm and short on storage, add a shelf with brackets over the tub (right). If storage needs are great, add a second shelf over the door.*

264 *Use hook-and-loop tape, attached to the under side of the sink, (right) as a quick way to skirt a sink and increase your storage possibilities. One section of the tape is glued to the sink while the the other is stitched to the sink skirt. Choose storage containers that stack.*

265 Combine open, to-the-ceiling shelves with drawers and cabinets to maximize storage options (left). Use an ottoman with a hinged top for extras.

266 Keep the bath neat and uncluttered (below left) with pull-out towel bars.

267 Be inspired by kitchen organizing (below left). Often used under kitchen sinks, hinged pull-down drawers are a plus in the bath, too. Even the clothes and towel bin pulls out.

268 Cut in a shelf for extra tissue storage and a magazine rack (below left) for a well-organized master bath.

269 Make every inch count with shallow shelves between wall studs (below). Use for necessities in a tiny bath.

ACCESSORIZE FOR MAXIMUM STORAGE

Search out objects of beauty and style for easy solutions to your bed and bath storage crunch. With the array of products on the market for organizing everyday grooming items and dressing accessories, you can shop for items that not only serve your needs but also work with the palette and mood of your rooms. Whether your mood is traditional, contemporary, or your own stylish mix, choose items that enhance as well as organize. Remember, too, the fun of finding new uses for old standbys, such as trunks and practical storage cubes. When space is tight, combine a vintage trunk at the foot of the bed, as in this loft bedroom, with cubes for bedside tables. If you can't find a trunk, use a pair of cubes at the foot of the bed. In the guest room, trunks are ideal to stash away blankets and pillows.

270 *Keep your hair dryer handy (top right) inside a handsome storage box. Use small boxes in complementary patterns and colors for easy-to-lose items such as earrings and pins.*

271 *Find new uses for interesting items such as this dough bowl (top opposite), transformed into a holder for washcloths or guest towels. Metal or wicker baskets work equally well for towels in a powder room or guest bath. Use a small pottery dish for soaps.*

272 *Look for unusual, innovative storage. This vintage knife box (middle opposite) keeps rolled socks neat and readily at hand.*

273 *Turn bathroom essentials into decorative accessories (lower opposite) with sturdy glass canisters topped by tiered cast aluminum lids. Each canister is 6 inches tall for generous storage. A matching aluminum tray adds to the organized look.*

274 *In a bedroom with little or no storage, expand your options with a decorative storage cube (right) with lift-off lid. Specialty home decorating stores and catalogs carry variations on this versatile piece.*

275 *When you need maximum storage for items such as hats and bulky duvets or quilts, add a curved-top antique trunk (right) at the foot of a bed. This look gives interesting contrast to the sleek space.*

NO LONGER ONLY FOR WRITING CHECKS or answering letters, home offices are where millions of us do at least some of our daily jobs. And home offices are still as necessary as ever for busy families who need a command central to coordinate personal paperwork, children's activities, and volunteer and community projects. Children and teens need their versions of offices, too, as quiet havens for homework and reading. Whether your goal is one multipurpose space or separate areas for your office needs, this chapter has storage

OFFICES AT HOME

solutions from architect-designed desks and built-ins to quick, easy, and affordable ways to organize with baskets, boxes, bins, and office supply components.

Turn a generously sized entry, as shown here, or a corner of your living room into a home office/library with floor-to-ceiling shelves. Add a library ladder to reach books on the top shelves. Use boxes or baskets if you need concealed storage.

TUCKING IN A HOME OFFICE

You do have space for a home office—even in a small house or apartment. If you occasionally bring work home from the office or simply need a place to pay bills, a corner of your bedroom, kitchen, or breakfast or dining room is ideal. If you choose the bedroom, you'll have a quiet retreat away from the household noise and activities. Or, if you need to be in the center of family activities, the kitchen allows you to keep an eye on multiple events and share computer time with the kids.

276 *Turn a window wall into a serene bedroom office (left) with a built-in desk with file drawers and storage cabinets topped by open glass shelves for contemporary-style display. Although such a view is inspiring, place a computer so the screen is side-lit, rather than back-lit, by a window.*

277 *When building or remodeling, consider the home office/bedroom combination (above). Here, a half-wall divides and defines areas and includes the space-saving conveniences of built-in drawers and nightstands on the bedroom side. The wall is also ideal for adjustable reading lamps as shown.*

278 *Include a built-in desk and built-in bookshelves (above) in the office side of your bedroom office. This arrangement saves space and visually blends a multifunction room. If you prefer a freestanding bookcase, paint it and your desk or work table to match your walls for a sleek look.*

279 Create a comfortable, computer-oriented kitchen office with a keyboard tray under your built-in desk (left). The proper height of the tray lessens stresses and strains from long hours at the screen, as important at home as at the office.

280 Take advantage of every square inch in your office corner. The kitchen office (left) includes both concealed storage in upper cabinets as well as open shelves. The lower desk drawer works well as a handy file drawer. Use baskets to organize your shelves and desktop as shown.

281 Have a cabinetmaker design and craft a pull-out file storage cabinet when you need serious office storage in the kitchen. This unit includes plywood dividers to organize magazines and open bins (left) for notebooks and papers. A bulletin board is a convenient way to keep notices, invitations, and to-do lists at hand.

282 Transform a small dining area into a home office with a pull-down, tambour-door built-in (left and above). The door pulls down to conceal the computer and keyboard. File drawers below and floor-to-ceiling cabinets keep papers, office supplies, and business records out of sight.

DE-CLUTTER YOUR WORK SPACE

When you need a down-to-business home office, think about storage with a stylish edge. If clients or customers meet you for business, your office should portray a professional image of organization and good taste. But even if your office is for your eyes only, it's part of your home. With proper planning and finishes, the space can be a busy office during the day and part of a family room or library at night and on the weekends. Even a hardworking office can have some fun, too.

283 Mix finishes and woods for handsome storage that sets the design of your home office (opposite). The contrast between the light natural finish and the black enamel gives a sleek contemporary note to plain plywood shelves finished with an edging strip.

284 To maximize storage, position a shelving/desk unit to create a corner (opposite below) as shown for extra display. This works as the room is large enough for space between the desk and the mirrored wall. Cabinet doors, with touch latches rather than pulls or levers, impart a sleek, contemporary look.

285 A serious office does not have to be dull or expensive. Instead, get the most look for the least buck with well-planned, creative concealed storage (below left and right). Constructed from plywood, these cabinet doors slide back and forward to create cubes that hide the computer, with hanging shelf and stacked open shelves.

286 Open, to-the-ceiling shelving for little-used items and pull-out drawers behind simply sleek doors keep the necessities hidden (below left and right). More storage is concealed behind doors under the desktop.

■STORAGE OPTIONS

■ **When built-ins don't meet your needs, look at freestanding office unit components. Home decorating catalogs, office furniture stores, home supply warehouses, and discount and home center stores are sources of units in a range of prices and styles. As an alternative, work with a local carpenter to have a unit built to your specific needs.**

■ **If your space is extremely limited, consider a retail, all-in-one computer table/storage unit that folds out from a freestanding wardrobe. Or, if you like the look of a wardrobe or armoire, have a cabinetmaker convert the piece into your own mini office.**

■ **Create your own storage desk unit by supporting a plywood desktop on two wooden filing cabinets. Purchase wooden storage cubes and place them on the ends of the top.**

■STORAGE OPTIONS

■ For instant storage, substitute wooden storage cubes or plastic crates or bins. Mix colors for a fun look. Plastic crates can be tied together for quick, inexpensive storage. Use units as room dividers when two children share a room.

■ Add wicker hampers or wicker trunks for quick storage. These are ideal for books and magazines as well as toys. Use plastic boxes or baskets to organize small toys, pencils, and other school supplies.

■ Organize desk drawers with plastic divider trays or boxes. This keeps school supplies, such as pencils and tape, always at hand. Color-code desk drawers by painting the fronts in different bright or pastel colors.

■ Add wall-mounted shelves or Shaker pegs when space is tight. Encourage reading with a night table with a shelf for books.

ENCOURAGE HOME STUDY

When your children are old enough for homework, they are ready for a home office. A quiet place, away from the distractions of television and family life, promotes good study habits. And adequate, accessible storage at least encourages, if not guarantees, the opportunity to learn neatness and order at an early age. Study centers for school-age children and teens don't have to be elaborate. A writing surface with proper lighting, a comfortable chair, and a few drawers for projects-in-progress and school supplies are all you need to get started.

287 Take advantage of every square inch of space in a child's bedroom with a built-in corner cabinet (opposite). Open shelves encourage kids to put away books and toys.

288 Build in a simple desk with a keyboard drawer (opposite) so it can be adapted for a computer. Include drawers for school papers, supplies, and memorabilia.

289 Turn a playroom into a home study/art center with a sturdy table and chairs (below). A table provides space needed for elementary and middle school projects.

290 Encourage neatness by color coding storage shelves in a built-in or freestanding unit (below). To avoid the danger of tipping over when loaded with heavy objects, bolt shelves securely to the wall.

291 Transform an unfinished cabinet, such as this armoire (above), into study and toy storage with cut-out plywood detailing and stock trim.

292 Paint in a lively color combination (above). Adapt the interior with low, divided shelves to promote an organized approach to homework time.

293 Create a simple study desk (above) with a painted chest and plywood top and side. Paint the pulls in contrasting colors; add decorative pulls for fun storage with style.

COMPARTMENTS FOR MAXIMUM STORAGE

When overwhelmed by piles of disorganized papers and overflowing boxes, turn to simple, efficient solutions. Organized, affordable options are as close as your neighborhood shopping center or home decorating catalog. Look at what's available at office supply stores, discount and home centers, and shops that specialize in storage and organizing products. And don't forget import and craft stores. Part of the fun of storage with style is finding new uses for items, such as baskets, boxes, tins, and even small trunks. If this appeals to you, search through your home and your own collections. Or visit flea markets and thrift, antique, or secondhand shops to find other ways to adapt your finds to your personal storage needs.

Decide what you have and what you need to create an attractive, organized space. A mix of new items, designed for storage, with vintage items can be just what you need to impart a personal feeling to your work space.

294 Put your basket collection to good use to organize papers and supplies on open shelves (right). Mix sizes and styles to adapt baskets to your particular storage and organizational needs and office supplies.

295 Substitute flat baskets for in and out boxes (right) as well as pencil and pen holders. Baskets with handles are particularly handy if you move between work surfaces. Look for baskets with dividers for quick organizing.

296 Have fun with baskets old and new. As you visit craft and antique shows, shop for sturdy split oak or twig baskets made by folk artists or interesting Native American baskets.

297 Use wicker trunks and hampers to store larger items. These are ideal to fit under work counters or desks.